THE ELEMENTS

Iodine

Leon Gray

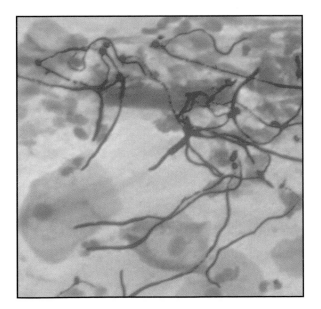

BENCHMARK BOOKS

MARSHALL CAVENDISH
NEW YORK

Benchmark Books
Marshall Cavendish
99 White Plains Road
Tarrytown, New York 10591

www.marshallcavendish.com

Library of Congress Cataloging-in-Publication Data

Gray, Leon, 1974–.
Iodine / Leon Gray.
p.   cm. — (The elements)
Includes index.

ISBN 0-7614-1812-1
1. Iodine—Juvenile literature. I. Title. II.
Elements (Benchmark Books)
QD181.I1G73 2005
546'.734—dc22

2004047644

Printed in China

Picture credits
Front Cover: Science Photo Library, Claude Nuridsany & Marie Perennou
Back Cover: Corbis, James Marshall

Art Explosion: 23t/r, 23c
Corbis: James L. Amos 18, Michael Freeman 11, James Marshall 12, Charles O'Rear 13, Alison Wright 24
Hemera: 23t/l
PHIL: 1, 20
PhotoDisc: Alex L Fradkin 3, 9
Science Photo Library: Andrew Lambert Photography 8, 14, 15, 16, 30, Martyn F. Chillmaid 21,
Mike Devlin 25, Russ Lappa 4, Claude Nuridsany & Marie Perennou 7; Oulette & Theroux, Publiphoto Library 27,
Alfred Pasieka 22, Philippe Plailly 26, Dagmar Schilling, Peter Arnold Inc. 19, Charles D Winters 17
University of Pennsylvania: Edgar Fahs Smith Collection 10

Series created by The Brown Reference Group plc.
Designed by Sarah Williams
www.brownreference.com

Contents

What is iodine?

Iodine exists as solid, blue-black crystals at standard room temperature and pressure.

Y ou may not realize it, but you are using iodine all the time. This slate-gray crystalline nonmetal is vital to your health. The human body needs a small amount of iodine to maintain the chemical processes, collectively called metabolism, going on inside cells. Iodine is equally important in medicine, where it is used as an antiseptic and for diagnosing and treating various cancers.

Iodine and its compounds are useful in many other ways, too. In industry, iodine is used to make dyes and a range of important organic (carbon-containing) chemicals. Photographers use a compound called silver iodide (AgI) to form images on photographic film. Biologists use iodine to stain the cell walls of plants and bacteria and to test substances for the presence of starch. Chemists use iodine as an indicator in chemical reactions. Physicists have developed powerful iodine lasers for use in industry and as weapons.

The iodine atom

Everything in the universe consists of tiny particles called atoms. Atoms are the building blocks of the elements. Chemists use powerful microscopes to study atoms, because atoms are too small to be seen by the naked eye. The period at the end of this sentence would cover 250 billion atoms.

When chemists looked closer at atoms, they discovered even smaller particles called protons, neutrons, and electrons. They found that the protons and neutrons cluster together in the dense nucleus at the center of the atom. The electrons revolve around the nucleus in a series of layers called electron shells.

The number of protons in the nucleus of an element is given by the atomic number. Iodine's atomic number is 53, so there are 53 protons in the nucleus of every iodine atom. No other element has this number of protons. Most of the time, atoms in an element have equal numbers of protons and electrons, so each iodine atom has 53 electrons revolving around the nucleus.

Every proton carries a tiny positive charge, and every electron carries a tiny negative charge. Neutrons are about the same size as protons, but they have no charge. The number of neutrons and protons in an atom gives the element its atomic mass. Iodine has an atomic mass of 127, so there are 74 neutrons in the nucleus of every iodine atom.

A reactive element

Iodine is a member of the halogen group of elements in the periodic table. The other halogens are fluorine, chlorine, bromine,

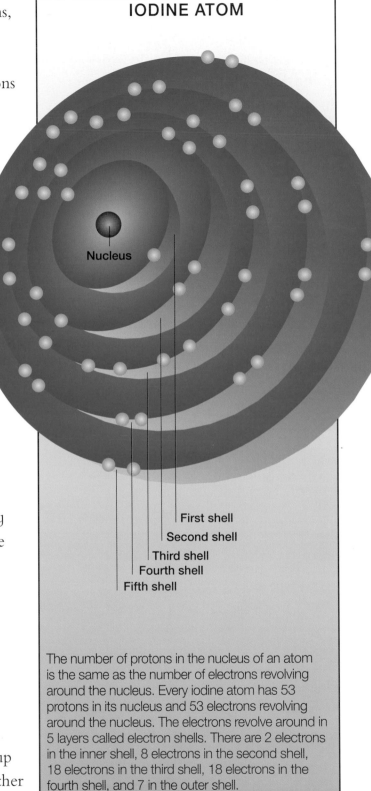

IODINE ATOM

Nucleus

First shell
Second shell
Third shell
Fourth shell
Fifth shell

The number of protons in the nucleus of an atom is the same as the number of electrons revolving around the nucleus. Every iodine atom has 53 protons in its nucleus and 53 electrons revolving around the nucleus. The electrons revolve around in 5 layers called electron shells. There are 2 electrons in the inner shell, 8 electrons in the second shell, 18 electrons in the third shell, 18 electrons in the fourth shell, and 7 in the outer shell.

and astatine. All the halogens are highly reactive, which means that they form compounds with other elements very easily. The arrangement of the electrons in the outer electron shell determines the reactivity of the halogens.

Atoms are most stable when they have full outer electron shells. Halogen atoms have seven electrons in their outer shells, with space for one more. When a halogen atom reacts with the atom of another element, it takes an electron from the other element to fill up the outer electron shell. When the halogen atom captures the electron, it has a negative charge. It is now called an anion. The element that loses the electron has a positive charge and is called a cation. This transfer of electrons forms bonds between the atoms, resulting in molecules and compounds.

DID YOU KNOW?

ATOMIC MASS NUMBER

The atomic mass number of an element is the number of particles in the nucleus. Most iodine atoms have 74 neutrons and 53 protons in their nuclei, so iodine's atomic mass number is 127. However, the actual mass of the atom is different because protons and neutrons differ in mass very slightly, and a small amount of mass is converted into energy and released when the nucleus is formed. The actual atomic mass of an iodine atom is 126.90447.

ATOMS AT WORK

Like other halogens, each iodine atom has seven electrons in its outer electron shell. Atoms are more stable if they have eight electrons in the outer electron shell.

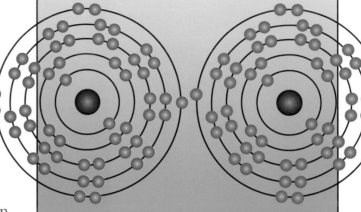

When iodine is found as an element, two iodine atoms have joined up to form a molecule. Each atom shares one electron with the other atom so that each one has eight electrons in its outer shell.

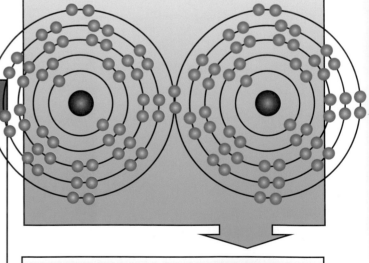

Iodine is a solid made up of pairs of iodine atoms, which are called diatomic molecules. The formula of diatomic iodine can be written like this:

$$I_2$$

Special characteristics

Iodine is a nonmetallic solid at room temperature, forming lustrous (shiny), blue-black crystals. Scientists take great care when they handle iodine in the laboratory. If a person touches the crystals, the iodine acts as an irritant and may cause painful rashes on the skin.

Sublimation

All substances exist in one of three states of matter—a solid, a liquid, or a gas. The atoms or molecules in a solid substance bind together into a rigid structure, giving the solid a fixed shape. In a liquid, the atoms or molecules are loosely bound, so they can move around to fit the shape of any container. Gases have no shape because the atoms or molecules are free to spread out in all directions.

When a solid substance is heated, the atoms or molecules absorb energy. Eventually, the atoms or molecules gain enough energy to break free from the rigid solid structure. The solid melts (at a temperature called the melting point) and turns into a liquid. If more heat is applied, the atoms or molecules eventually gain enough energy to break free from the surface of the liquid. The liquid boils (at a temperature called the boiling point) and turns into a gas.

Gently heating solid iodine crystals releases the element as a purple gas. The direct transition from a solid to a gas is called sublimation.

DID YOU KNOW?

IODINE ISOTOPES

Elements have different versions of their atoms, called isotopes, that contain different numbers of neutrons in the nucleus. Some isotopes are radioactive, which means they break down into other elements. In nature, every iodine atom has 74 neutrons in the nucleus. This version of iodine is called a stable isotope, because it does not decay easily. Chemists have made a total of fourteen unstable iodine isotopes in the laboratory. Many of them are very useful in medicine.

Iodine does not readily dissolve in water, but it will dissolve in a chemical called cyclohexane to make a violet solution. This solution forms a layer on top of the water, because cyclohexane and water do not mix.

Iodine exists as solid crystals at room temperature. If the crystals are heated gently, the iodine changes directly from a solid to a violet gas, without turning into a liquid. This process is called sublimation. It occurs because the heat gives the iodine molecules enough energy to jump free of the surface of the crystals. Iodine crystals do melt eventually, but only when the temperature reaches 236 °F (113.5 °C).

Solubility

Solutions consist of a solvent—the dissolving substance—and a solute—the substance that is dissolved. In a solution, the solute and solvent completely mix.

A solute dissolves best when its particles are attracted to the solvent at least as strongly as they are to each other.

Iodine dissolves in some substances but not in others. For example, iodine dissolves in a chemical called cyclohexane (C_6H_{12}) to form a violet solution. But iodine does not readily dissolve in water. This is because the forces that hold the water molecules together are much stronger than the forces that hold the iodine molecules together. When iodine is added to water, the forces between the iodine molecules cannot overcome the forces between the water molecules. The iodine and water molecules do not completely mix. When iodine is added to cyclohexane, the forces that hold the iodine molecules together are no stronger than the forces between the cyclohexane molecules. The two chemicals mix freely.

IODINE FACTS

- Chemical symbol: I
- Atomic number: 53
- Atomic weight: 127
- Melting point: 236 °F (113.5 °C)
- Boiling point: 363 °F (184 °C)
- Isotopes: 1 natural isotope (around 14 artificial isotopes)
- Name's origin: The word *iodine* comes from the Greek *ioeides*, meaning "violet"

Iodine in nature

Iodine is never found as a pure element in nature. It is always combined with other elements as compounds. Traces of iodine compounds are sometimes found inside rocks. However, there is very little useful iodine in rocks—about 0.5 parts per million of Earth's crust.

Iodine also exists as sodium iodate ($NaIO_3$) and calcium iodate ($Ca(IO_3)_2$). Both compounds are found as trace impurities in deposits of Chilean saltpeter (sodium nitrate; $NaNO_3$). Some iodine on Earth occurs as ions in seawater. Seawater contains about one thousandth of an ounce of iodine ions per ton of seawater (50 milligrams per tonne). Salt water found underground contains higher concentrations of iodine ions.

Iodine in animals and plants

Most living things contain trace amounts of iodine, because it is essential for good health. Some animals and plants that live in the sea absorb a lot of iodine from the seawater. For example, codfish absorb iodine into their livers. Iodine is also collected in sea plants, such as kelp, and shellfish, such as oysters.

Sea plants called kelp absorb the iodine ions found in seawater. Kelp is an important source of iodine.

The discovery of iodine

The discovery of iodine came about by chance in 1811. Bernard Courtois (1777–1838) trained as a pharmacist in the French army. Later, he left to join his father, who had set up a company making saltpeter, or sodium nitrate ($NaNO_3$). Saltpeter was one of the ingredients for making gunpowder. Gunpowder was very much in demand at the time, because the French army was fighting the Napoleonic Wars.

Courtois made saltpeter by mixing seaweed ash with sulfuric acid (H_2SO_4). One day Courtois added too much acid to the seaweed ash. He noticed that a violet vapor escaped and condensed, forming dark blue-black crystals. Courtois performed many experiments on the crystals and published his results in 1813.

Competition among chemists

Although Courtois may have recognized that he had discovered a new element, his work fell short of proving it. Two great chemists of the time, Joseph-Louis Gay-Lussac (1778–1850) from France and Humphry Davy (1778–1829) of Britain, seized on Courtois's discovery. They set about trying to prove that the crystals were in fact a new chemical element.

This engraving of Joseph-Louis Gay-Lussac dates from 1824. Gay-Lussac and Humphry Davy were bitter rivals. Both chemists claimed to have discovered that iodine is an element.

Davy was a talented chemist, who had already discovered the elements boron, potassium, and sodium. In 1810, he added chlorine to this list. Davy was traveling through France on a scientific tour when he heard about Courtois's work. Quickly, Davy set up a laboratory to study the new substance. Davy soon discovered that the new substance had similar properties to chlorine. In November 1813, Davy visited Paris. There he performed a series of public experiments to prove that the substance was in fact a new element.

Gay-Lussac was not very impressed with Davy's work, so he studied the new substance in greater depth. On August 1, 1814, he announced the results of his experiments to the National Institute and later published them in the French chemistry journal *Annales de chimie*.

Many scientists still credit Davy for figuring out that iodine was an element. It is fitting that iodine is still called by the name that Gay-Lussac chose for it, taken from the Greek word *ioeides*, which means "violet-colored."

The manufacture of saltpeter (shown below) for gunpowder led to the discovery of iodine in 1811.

DID YOU KNOW?

DISCOVERING THE HALOGENS

Swedish chemist Carl Wilhelm Scheele (1742–1786) isolated the first halogen, chlorine, in 1774, but he did not recognize it to be a new element. British chemist Humphry Davy proved this to be the case in 1810. Davy also played a part in fluorine's discovery. In 1813, Davy suggested that this element existed in a compound he was studying. It took another 73 years for French chemist Henri Moissan (1852–1907) to prove him right. Bromine's discovery came in 1826, when French chemist Antoine-Jérôme Balard isolated the element from seaweed. Astatine was the last halogen to be discovered. This was achieved by Italian-born U.S. physicist Emilio Segrè (1905–1989) and his colleagues in 1940.

Producing iodine

Kelp is farmed off the shore of Okinawa on the Ryukyu Islands in Japan. Kelp is the raw material for the commercial production of iodine. It is also a popular food item in Japan.

For many years, the most important commercial source of iodine came from the saltpeter beds of Chile. There, iodine is found in the form of two iodine compounds—sodium iodate ($NaIO_3$) and calcium iodate ($Ca(IO_3)_2$). Both compounds are found in small amounts in unrefined Chilean saltpeter (sodium nitrate; $NaNO_3$) deposits. In Chile, iodine is made as a by-product of the saltpeter industry. Saltpeter is used as the raw material to make explosives and fertilizers.

To separate the pure iodine from its compounds, the saltpeter is first dissolved in boiling water. As the solution cools, the saltpeter forms white crystals. This leaves a solution rich in iodate ions (IO_3^-).

The solution is divided into two parts. Sodium hydrogen sulfite ($NaHSO_4$) is added to the first part of the iodate-rich solution. This changes the iodate ions in the solution to iodide ions (I^-). At this point, sodium carbonate ($NaCO_3$) is added to stop the reaction. The iodide solution is then mixed with the second part of the iodate solution.

The iodate ions then convert all the iodide ions to pure iodine. A solid product, containing up to 80 percent iodine, is collected and washed with water. The solid is then pressed into blocks and heated to remove the excess water.

Natural brines

Natural brines (salt water) are important sources of iodine today. Brines from California, Indonesia, and northern Italy are particularly rich in iodine. The first step in the extraction is to filter the brine to remove impurities, such as clay and sand. The water is then passed through containers containing bundles of copper wires. The iodine in the brine reacts with the copper, forming copper iodide (Cu_2I_2). This compound is separated from the solution by filtering, leaving the solid copper iodide. After the copper iodide is washed, it is finely ground and heated with potassium carbonate (K_2CO_3) to produce potassium iodide (KI). Free iodine is then obtained by reacting the potassium iodide with chlorine gas (Cl_2).

Nitrates, such as saltpeter, found in the Atacama Desert in Chile contain small amounts of iodine.

Iodine from seaweed

The iodine in seawater is too dilute to recover economically, so chemists use another source of iodine—sea plants such as kelp. Kelp is rich in iodine because it absorbs the element from seawater. Britain, France, and Japan are the world's leading producers of iodine from this source.

To recover the iodine from the kelp, the plants are shredded and mixed with water. The solution is filtered, which leaves a solid rich in iodide ions. When chlorine gas is bubbled through the water, a chemical reaction takes place. The chlorine molecules take electrons from the iodide ions to form chloride ions (Cl^-). The iodide ions lose the electrons, forming a solution of elemental iodine. The iodine is separated by boiling the solution in a closed vessel. The iodine vaporizes, cools at the top of the chamber, and then condenses to form solid iodine.

DID YOU KNOW?

IODINE PRODUCERS
Each year, around 18,000 tons (16,300 tonnes) of iodine is produced worldwide. Japan supplies more than 7,000 tons (6,300 tonnes), making it the top iodine-producing country in the world. Chile is the second-highest iodine producer. It supplies around 6,250 tons (5,650 tonnes) each year. Other important iodine-producing countries include Britain, France, Indonesia, Italy, and the United States.

Chemistry and compounds

How reactive a halogen is depends on the way in which the atoms attract electrons from other elements. Atoms are stable when they have eight electrons in the outer electron shell. All the halogens have seven electrons in the outer shell. Since they need only one more electron to fill up the outer shell, all the halogens, including iodine, are extremely reactive.

Trends in reactivity

Halogens get less reactive as their atomic mass increases and they get heavier. Fluorine is the most reactive halogen. It reacts with almost all of the other elements, including the other halogens. Chlorine is the next most reactive halogen, then bromine, iodine, and finally astatine, which is the least reactive. How do chemists explain this trend in reactivity?

The answer lies in the size of the halogen's atoms. As the atomic mass of a halogen atom increases, so does its size. Fluorine has the smallest atoms, so the outer electron shell is very close to the positive nucleus. Iodine has much larger atoms, so the outer electron shell is farther away from the nucleus. When a halogen reacts, it captures an electron to fill up the outer shell. Fluorine's nucleus is close to the outer electron shell, so its positive charge attracts

The reactivity of the three halogen elements chlorine (Cl_2), bromine (Br_2), and iodine (I_2) decreases from left to right.

Chlorine

Bromine

PYREX

Iodine

When chlorine gas passes through a clear solution of potassium iodide, chlorine atoms replace the iodine atoms in the potassium iodide. A brown solution of elemental iodine forms in the potassium chloride.

electrons very strongly. Iodine's nucleus is farther away, so it attracts electrons less strongly. This explains why iodine is less reactive than most halogens.

Chemical reactions called displacement reactions—reactions in which one element displaces another in a compound—show this change in reactivity. For example, iodine atoms steal electrons from potassium atoms to form potassium iodide (KI). But fluorine, chlorine, and bromine are more reactive than iodine. Any one of these

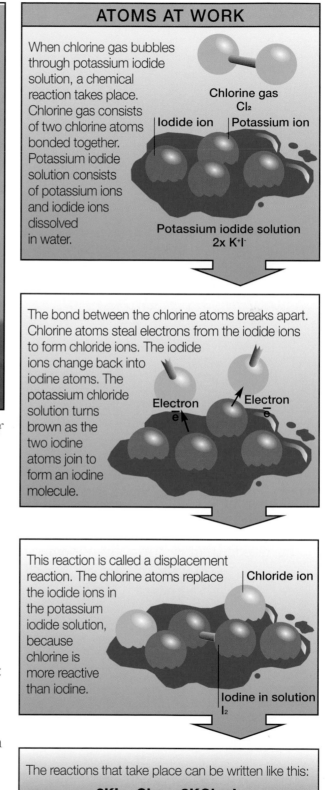

ATOMS AT WORK

When chlorine gas bubbles through potassium iodide solution, a chemical reaction takes place. Chlorine gas consists of two chlorine atoms bonded together. Potassium iodide solution consists of potassium ions and iodide ions dissolved in water.

Chlorine gas
Cl_2

Iodide ion   Potassium ion

Potassium iodide solution
$2x\ K^+I^-$

The bond between the chlorine atoms breaks apart. Chlorine atoms steal electrons from the iodide ions to form chloride ions. The iodide ions change back into iodine atoms. The potassium chloride solution turns brown as the two iodine atoms join to form an iodine molecule.

Electron $\bar{e}$ Electron $\bar{e}$

This reaction is called a displacement reaction. The chlorine atoms replace the iodide ions in the potassium iodide solution, because chlorine is more reactive than iodine.

Chloride ion

Iodine in solution
I_2

The reactions that take place can be written like this:

$$2KI + Cl_2 \rightarrow 2KCl + I_2$$

15

A student performs a chemical reaction in which a purple iodine-containing solution is used to indicate the progress of a reaction. When the reaction is complete, the iodine solution turns colorless.

The oxidation state is a number that tells chemists how many electrons an atom has lost or gained. When an iodine atom steals an electron from another atom, its oxidation state is given as –1. In this case, the negative number means that the iodine atom has gained one electron. Iodine has an oxidation state of –1 in the compound potassium iodide. Potassium loses one electron, so it has an oxidation state of +1.

Covalent bonds

Iodine can also have positive oxidation states in some compounds and ions. These compounds and ions exist because iodine shares electrons with other elements, forming what are known as covalent (shared electron) bonds. In the iodate ion (IO_3^-), for example, the iodine atom forms a covalent bond with three oxygen atoms,

halogens can steal electrons from iodine ions, replacing the iodine in the potassium compound. For example, potassium fluoride (KF) forms when fluorine replaces iodine in the potassium iodide.

Oxidation and reduction

Substances that take electrons from other substances are known as oxidizing agents. When iodine steals an electron from another element, the iodine is reduced. The element that loses electrons is oxidized.

sharing six electrons from its outer shell. This would indicate that the oxidation state is +6. However, iodine has seven electrons in its outer shell. This spare electron gives the iodine atom in the ion an overall oxidation state of +5.

Since the iodine atom is very big, it comes into contact with more oxygen atoms, forming covalent bonds. Some compounds have as many as six oxygen atoms around a central iodine atom.

Iodine in the test tube sublimes from blue-black crystals to a violet gas. This gas reacts with zinc in the glass flask to produce zinc iodide (ZnI₂).

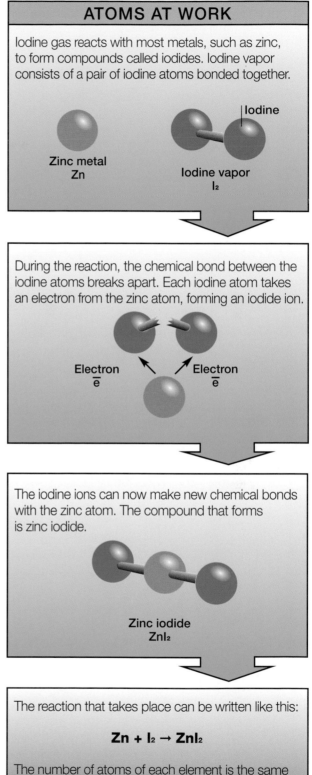

ATOMS AT WORK

Iodine gas reacts with most metals, such as zinc, to form compounds called iodides. Iodine vapor consists of a pair of iodine atoms bonded together.

Iodine

Zinc metal
Zn

Iodine vapor
I_2

During the reaction, the chemical bond between the iodine atoms breaks apart. Each iodine atom takes an electron from the zinc atom, forming an iodide ion.

Electron
$\overline{e}$

Electron
$\overline{e}$

The iodine ions can now make new chemical bonds with the zinc atom. The compound that forms is zinc iodide.

Zinc iodide
ZnI_2

The reaction that takes place can be written like this:

$$Zn + I_2 \rightarrow ZnI_2$$

The number of atoms of each element is the same on both sides of the equation.

How iodine is used

Chemicals used to "develop" a photograph turn silver iodide into metallic silver, forming an image on the paper. Sodium thiosulfate ($Na_2S_2O_3$), or hypo, is then used to fix the image permanently.

Iodine played a vital role in the development of modern photography. Joseph Nicéphore Niépce (1765–1833) and Louis-Jacques-Mandé Daguerre (1787–1851) from France developed the first photographic process in the 1820s. They used iodine to form images on silver-coated copper plates.

Daguerre and Niépce placed a silver-coated plate in a chamber filled with iodine gas. The iodine gas reacted with the silver, forming a layer of light-sensitive silver iodide (AgI) on the surface of the plate. Then they used a simple camera, called a camera obscura, to form a picture on the plate. When light from the camera hit the silver iodide, it turned the silver ions into metallic silver. Daguerre and Niépce then dipped the plate in mercury vapor. The mercury attached to the areas of the plate exposed to the light to reveal the image. These early photographs were called daguerrotypes.

Photography improved rapidly in the nineteenth century. In 1841, British inventor William Fox Talbot (1800–1877) formed negative images on paper soaked in silver iodide. These negatives could be used to produce more than one copy of the positive image. Tougher celluloid film was invented shortly after.

Reactions between hot oxygen and iodine gas make light used in strong chemical lasers.

Today, the silver iodide in photographic film and paper has largely been replaced by silver bromide (AgBr), which is more sensitive to light. However, silver iodide is still used to make the film used to form X-ray images in hospitals.

Cloud seeding

Silver iodide has another important use. In some areas, scientists "seed" clouds with sodium iodide particles to make rain when it would not normally fall. Clouds consist of millions of tiny water droplets. The water falls as rain if the droplets join together to form heavier droplets. This can only occur if particles, such as dust or pollutants, are present in the atmosphere. In the cold conditions of a cloud, the water droplets

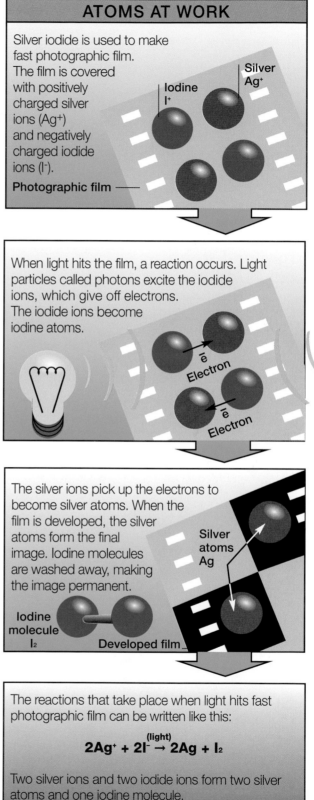

ATOMS AT WORK

Silver iodide is used to make fast photographic film. The film is covered with positively charged silver ions (Ag^+) and negatively charged iodide ions (I^-).

Iodine I^+
Silver Ag^+
Photographic film

When light hits the film, a reaction occurs. Light particles called photons excite the iodide ions, which give off electrons. The iodide ions become iodine atoms.

$\bar{e}$ **Electron**
$\bar{e}$ **Electron**

The silver ions pick up the electrons to become silver atoms. When the film is developed, the silver atoms form the final image. Iodine molecules are washed away, making the image permanent.

Silver atoms Ag
Iodine molecule I_2
Developed film

The reactions that take place when light hits fast photographic film can be written like this:

$$2Ag^+ + 2I^- \xrightarrow{\text{(light)}} 2Ag + I_2$$

Two silver ions and two iodide ions form two silver atoms and one iodine molecule.

form small ice crystals on the surfaces of these particles. More water vapor freezes onto the crystals, which become heavy and eventually fall as rain. The crystal structure of the silver iodide particles is similar to the ice crystals that form in clouds. The water droplets coat the silver iodide particles with ice and grow as if the particle were a natural ice particle.

Dyes and stains

Iodine is a colorful element, and it forms some equally colorful compounds. As a result, dye and ink manufacturers use

A gram test has stained these bacteria a deep violet, which means they are gram-positive bacteria.

> ## DID YOU KNOW?
>
> ### SCHOENBEIN PAPER
> In 1839 Swiss chemist Christian Schoenbein developed a test to measure the level of ozone in the atmosphere. He spread a mixture of starch, potassium iodide, and water on to a piece of filter paper. Left outside, ozone in the air oxidizes the potassium iodide on the paper to produce iodine. The iodine then reacts with the starch, staining the paper purple. The darker the color, the more ozone is present in the atmosphere.

iodine and its compounds to make a range of dyes and the superbright colors of fluorescent paints. An iodine dye is also used in biology to tell different bacteria apart. In a procedure called the gram test,

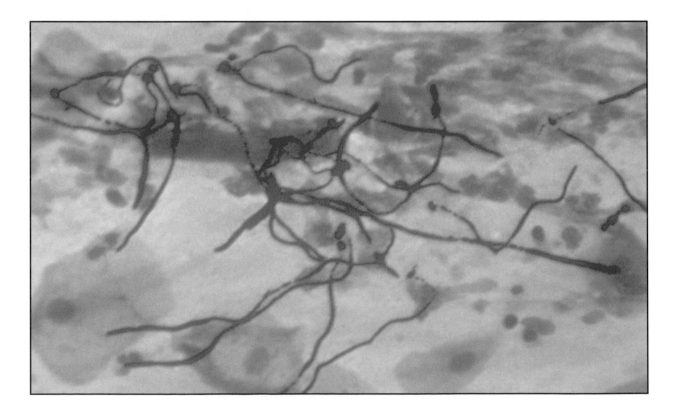

bacteria are treated with an iodine dye. Bacteria that stain deep violet are called gram-positive bacteria. Bacteria that stain pink are called gram-negative bacteria.

Doctors use the gram test to decide which antibiotic should be used to treat a bacterial infection. Gram-positive bacteria respond well to penicillin. Gram-negative bacteria are better treated with antibiotics such as streptomycin.

Iodine analysis

Iodine and its compounds have many uses in analytical chemistry. A blue-black color forms when iodine is added to a substance that contains starch. This is the standard chemical test for starch. Iodine is also used to measure the unsaturation of fats and oils. Unsaturated fats and oils contain carbon atoms that are joined by double

A blue-black color forms when iodine is added to a solution containing starch.

bonds. Iodine is attracted to the double bonds in unsaturated fats and oils. The more iodine taken up by a fat or oil, the less saturated it is. Chemists assign fats and oils an iodine value, which is the number of grams of iodine that is taken up by 100 grams (3.5 ounces) of the fat or oil.

Other applications

Iodine and its compounds have many other uses. For example, tungsten iodide is used to make the filaments in electric light bulbs. Iodine compounds are also used to purify transition metals. Others are used as catalysts (helper substances) in the chemical industry.

SEE FOR YOURSELF

STARCH IN FOODS

You will need a bottle of iodine solution to do this experiment. You may have to ask your parents to buy you a bottle from the pharmacy.

Iodine turns black when it comes in contact with starch. Test different food items, such as bread, cheese, eggs, ham, and potatoes, to see if they contain starch. Just put a drop of iodine on the food and watch the color change.

Warning: Iodine is poisonous and may stain skin and clothes. Do not eat food that you have tested with the iodine solution.

Iodine and health

Iodine is an essential trace element for most living organisms. In humans and other mammals, iodine is concentrated in the thyroid gland found in the neck. The thyroid gland uses iodine to make proteins called hormones. The thyroid gland makes two important iodine-containing hormones: thyroxine and triiodothyronine. The body uses these hormones to control growth and regulate the chemical processes inside cells.

Most people get all the iodine they need from their food. Important sources of iodine include fish, nuts, seaweed, and shellfish. In some countries, however, particularly in mountainous regions and

The human body contains about 0.0005 ounces (14 milligrams) of iodine. Almost all of this iodine is found in the thyroid gland.

places far away from the sea, people do not eat enough iodine-rich food. Iodine deficiencies cause serious health problems.

Iodine deficiencies

When the body does not get the iodine it needs, the thyroid gland cannot make enough thyroxine and triiodothyronine.

DID YOU KNOW?

IODIZED SALT

In some countries such as Canada, the Netherlands, Switzerland, and the United States, people do not get enough iodine from their food. Since iodine deficiency causes health problems, officials in those countries have decided to add iodine (usually in the form of potassium iodide; KI) to table salt (sodium chloride; NaCl). The World Health Organization recommends that iodized salt contains one molecule of iodine for every 100,000 salt molecules. In the United States, iodized salt contains one iodine molecule in every 10,000 molecules of salt.

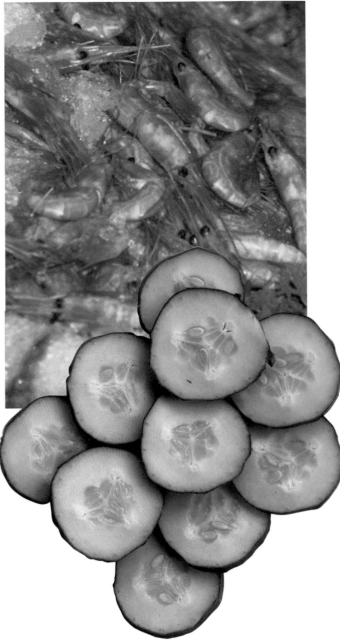

Some important sources of iodine include nuts such as almonds (above), shellfish such as shrimps (top right), and fruits such as cucumbers (right).

This results in a hormonal disorder called hypothyroidism. A goiter is the most common symptom of hypothyroidism. Since there is a lack of iodine in the body, the thyroid gland works very hard to maintain the production of thyroid hormones. The overactive thyroid gland enlarges, which results in a goiter—a large swelling in the neck. In some cases, the thyroid gland may swell up to two or three times its normal size. Usually, goiters are not too serious. People may have some difficulty breathing and swallowing, but they can continue to lead a normal life. Treatment will usually involve taking iodine supplements and an iodine-rich diet.

Some cases of goiters, called sporadic goiters, appear in places where there is plenty of iodine in food. Doctors think that sporadic goiters are caused by chemicals that stop the body from absorbing iodine. These chemicals are found in vegetables such as cabbage.

Prolonged cases of iodine deficiency may result in a condition known as myxedema. Symptoms of myxedema include dry, puffy skin; hair loss; swollen lips; sluggishness; muscular weakness; and weight gain. Myxedema can be treated by hormone therapy, using artificial hormones to replace the missing thyroxine and triiodothyronine.

If a woman does not eat foods rich in iodine during pregnancy, the developing fetus may suffer from hypothyroidism. This may continue once the baby has been born. Urgent treatment is required, because the baby will grow up suffering from cretinism. Cretins have stunted growth and are mentally handicapped.

This woman has a large swelling, or a goiter, on her neck. Goiters may result from an overactive thyroid gland, a lack of dietary iodine, or thyroid cancer.

DID YOU KNOW?

GRAVES' DISEASE

Graves' disease occurs when the thyroid gland produces more thyroid hormones than the body needs. A goiter and protruding eyeballs are the most obvious symptoms, but the high levels of hormones also affect the heart, producing a rapid, irregular heartbeat. Other symptoms include insomnia, weak muscles, nervousness, and weight loss. Radioactive iodine is often used to treat Graves' disease. It is taken up by the thyroid gland and destroys some, but not all, of the cells. Usually, enough tissue remains for the thyroid to continue working properly. In severe cases, however, surgery to remove all or part of the thyroid gland is the only option.

Iodine in medicine

About 50 percent of the world's supply of iodine is used for medical purposes. Some of this iodine is used as a dietary supplement in the prevention of iodine-deficiency diseases. Iodine is also used as a mild antiseptic in the form of tincture of iodine—a solution of iodine and ethanol. Tincture of iodine is used to sterilize minor

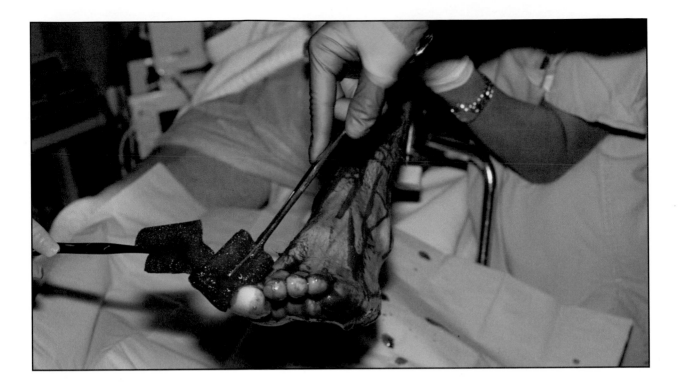

A patient's foot is swabbed with an iodine antiseptic (colored red) before surgery. The antiseptic kills any bacteria on the skin, which minimizes the risk of infection during the operation.

cuts and grazes. It kills microorganisms, such as bacteria and fungi, that would otherwise cause an infection. Iodine antiseptics are also used to sterilize the skin before surgery.

Doctors use iodine to diagnose cervical cancer. First, iodine is used to stain the woman's cervix (a part of the reproductive system). The doctor then uses a colposcope (an imaging device that allows doctors to look inside the body) to examine the stained cells. Iodine stains the cancer cells a dark brown or black.

Iodine and X rays

X rays are used to take pictures of the inside of the body. Different parts of the body affect X rays in different ways. X rays cannot pass through hard tissue, such as bone and teeth. These show up as white areas on the X-ray film. X rays pass through the lungs easily, because they are filled with air. The lungs show up as black areas on the X-ray film. Soft tissues, such as the heart or liver, show up as a gray color on the film, because they each absorb X rays by about the same amount.

Doctors often inject iodine compounds into the body to take clearer X rays of soft tissues. X rays cannot pass through iodine, so any iodine compounds in the body show up as white areas on the X-ray film.

Radioactive iodine

A scientist uses a protective "glove box" to prepare a radioactive iodine isotope for use in hospitals.

Unlike most other elements, there is only one isotope of iodine that is stable enough to be found widely in nature. This form of iodine is called iodine-127. The number 127 stands for the number of protons plus the number of neutrons in the nucleus. Since all iodine atoms must contain 53 protons, iodine-127 atoms contain 74 neutrons in the nucleus.

Decay

However, there are other iodine isotopes. They have different numbers of neutrons in the nucleus, making them unstable. Unstable isotopes are described as being radioactive. This means that they break down, or decay, forming atoms of entirely different elements. As they decay, the nuclei of radioactive isotopes also release small, fast-moving particles and huge amounts of heat, light, and other forms of radiation.

Iodine isotopes

One radioactive iodine isotope is called iodine-129. These atoms are produced naturally when another radioactive element—the rare gas xenon—decays in the atmosphere. It is also made by radioactive activity deep inside Earth's crust. As well as occurring naturally, larger quantities of I-129 are made during the decay of uranium-238, a metal used in nuclear power plants.

Other unstable isotopes of iodine are made artificially. Scientists fire neutrons at stable iodine atoms. A few of the neutrons stick to the nuclei making a new isotope. The longest-lasting artificial isotope of this kind is called iodine-131. Like all other radioactive substances, iodine isotopes have a half-life. This is a measure of how long it takes for half of the isotope nuclei to decay. Isotopes that are more unstable have shorter half-lives. I-129 has a half-life of 17 million years, while the half life of I-131 is just eight days.

Treating disease

Iodine, including the radioactive isotopes, is absorbed by the thyroid gland in the body. I-131 is used to treat tumors in the thyroid gland. The patient swallows some of the isotope. The iodine travels to the diseased thyroid. The radiation produced by the isotope then destroys the tumor.

Tracing radiation

Iodine-129 is produced by nuclear power plants, and it is used as a tracer to detect how much radiation has leaked into the air or water. Scientists measure how much I-129 there is in the area and compare it to the amount of non-radioactive I-127.

Where an accident has caused radioactive materials to leak out, the proportion of I-129 is much higher than normal. A test of the iodine in the thyroid gland can tell people how much radiation they have been exposed to after nuclear accidents.

Since radioactive iodine can cause cancer in the thyroid, people who are involved in a nuclear accident must take potassium iodate tablets as soon as possible. This loads the thyroid with non-radioactive iodine, stopping any of the dangerous radioactive isotopes from being stored inside the body.

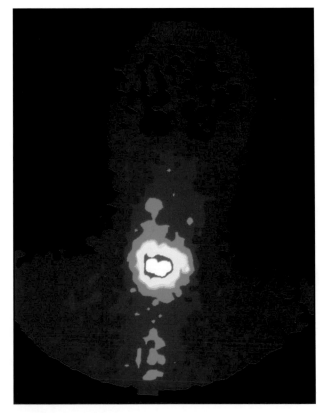

The bright area in the center of this scan shows a tumor in the thyroid gland.

Periodic table

Everything in the universe consists of combinations of substances called elements. Elements are the building blocks of matter. They are made of tiny atoms, which are too small to see.

The character of an atom depends on how many even tinier particles called protons there are in its center, or nucleus. An element's atomic number is the same as the number of its protons.

Scientists have found around 110 different elements. About 90 elements occur naturally on Earth. The rest have been made in laboratories.

All the chemical elements are set out on a chart called the periodic table. This lists all the elements in order according to their atomic number.

The elements at the left of the table are metals. Those at the right are nonmetals. Between the metals and the nonmetals are the metalloids, which sometimes act like metals and sometimes like nonmetals.

● On the left of the table are the alkali metals. These elements have just one electron in their outer shells.

● Elements get more reactive as you go down a group.

● On the right of the periodic table are the noble gases. These elements have full outer shells.

● The number of electrons orbiting the nucleus increases down each group.

● Elements in the same group have the same number of electrons in their outer shells.

● The transition metals are in the middle of the table, between Groups II and III.

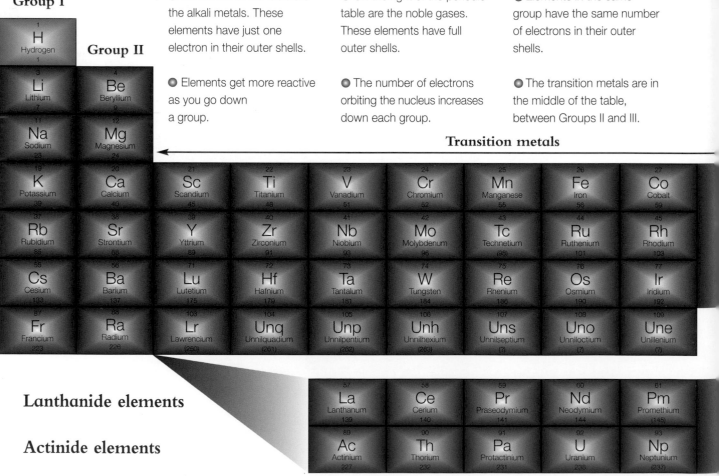

Group I

Group II

Transition metals

Lanthanide elements

Actinide elements

The horizontal rows of the table are called periods. As you go across a period, the atomic number increases by one from each element to the next. The vertical columns are called groups. Elements get heavier as you go down a group. All the elements in a group have the same number of electrons in their outer shells. This means they react in similar ways.

The transition metals fall between Groups II and III. Their electron shells fill up in an unusual way. The lanthanide elements and the actinide elements are set apart from the main table to make it easier to read. All the lanthanide elements and the actinide elements are quite rare.

Iodine in the table

Iodine is one of the halogens in Group VII of the periodic table. Like all the other halogens, iodine has seven electrons in its outer electron shell, making it a very reactive element. Iodine reacts with most metals and some nonmetals to form a range of different compounds. Some of these compounds are very useful.

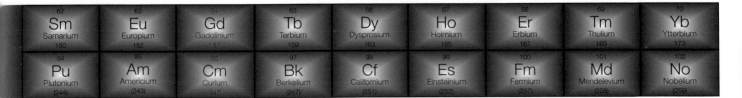

■ Metals
■ Metalloids (semimetals)
■ Nonmetals

53
I
Iodine
127

Atomic (proton) number
Symbol
Name
Atomic mass

Group III	Group IV	Group V	Group VI	Group VII	Group VIII
					2 He Helium 4
5 B Boron 11	6 C Carbon 12	7 N Nitrogen 14	8 O Oxygen 16	9 F Fluorine 19	10 Ne Neon 20
13 Al Aluminum 27	14 Si Silicon 28	15 P Phosphorus 31	16 S Sulfur 32	17 Cl Chlorine 35	18 Ar Argon 40

28 Ni Nickel 59	29 Cu Copper 64	30 Zn Zinc 65	31 Ga Gallium 70	32 Ge Germanium 73	33 As Arsenic 75	34 Se Selenium 79	35 Br Bromine 80	36 Kr Krypton 84
46 Pd Palladium 106	47 Ag Silver 108	48 Cd Cadmium 112	49 In Indium 115	50 Sn Tin 119	51 Sb Antimony 122	52 Te Tellurium 128	53 I Iodine 127	54 Xe Xenon 131
78 Pt Platinum 195	79 Au Gold 197	80 Hg Mercury 201	81 Tl Thallium 204	82 Pb Lead 207	83 Bi Bismuth 209	84 Po Polonium (209)	85 At Astatine (210)	86 Rn Radon (222)

62 Sm Samarium 150	63 Eu Europium 152	64 Gd Gadolinium 157	65 Tb Terbium 159	66 Dy Dysprosium 163	67 Ho Holmium 165	68 Er Erbium 167	69 Tm Thulium 169	70 Yb Ytterbium 173
94 Pu Plutonium (244)	95 Am Americium (243)	96 Cm Curium (247)	97 Bk Berkelium (247)	98 Cf Californium (251)	99 Es Einsteinium (252)	100 Fm Fermium (257)	101 Md Mendelevium (258)	102 No Nobelium (259)

Chemical reactions

Chemical reactions are going on all the time—candles burn, nails rust, and food is digested. Some reactions involve just two substances, others many more. But whenever a reaction takes place, at least one substance is changed.

In a chemical reaction, the atoms do not change. A hydrogen atom remains a hydrogen atom; an iodine atom remains an iodine atom. But they join together in new combinations to form new molecules.

Writing an equation

Chemical reactions can be described by writing down the atoms and molecules before and after the reaction. Since the atoms stay the same, the number of atoms before will be the same as the number of atoms after. Chemists write the reaction as a chemical equation. Equations are a quick and easy way of showing what happens during a chemical reaction.

Making it balance

When the numbers of each atom on both sides of the equation are equal, the equation is balanced. If the numbers are not equal, something is wrong. So the chemist adjusts the number of atoms involved until the equation does balance.

Aluminum reacts with iodine to produce aluminum iodide ($(AlI_3)_2$).

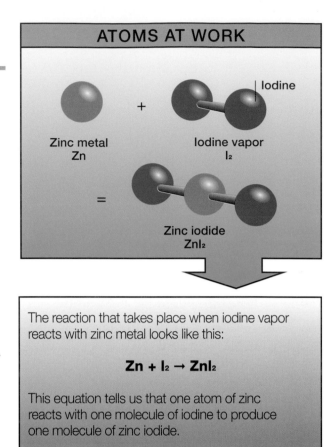

ATOMS AT WORK

Zinc metal
Zn

+

Iodine vapor
I_2

Iodine

=

Zinc iodide
ZnI_2

The reaction that takes place when iodine vapor reacts with zinc metal looks like this:

$$Zn + I_2 \rightarrow ZnI_2$$

This equation tells us that one atom of zinc reacts with one molecule of iodine to produce one molecule of zinc iodide.

Glossary

atom: The smallest part of an element having all the properties of that element. Each atom is less than a millionth of an inch in diameter.

atomic mass number: The number of protons and neutrons in an atom.

atomic number: The number of protons in an atom.

bond: The sharing or exchanging of electrons between atoms that holds them together to form molecules.

brine: Water with a large amount of salt dissolved in it.

compound: A substance made of atoms of more than one element. The atoms are held together by chemical bonds.

condense: To turn from a gas into a liquid.

crystal: A solid consisting of a repeating pattern of atoms, ions, or molecules.

electron: A tiny particle with a negative charge. Electrons are found inside atoms, where they move around the nucleus in layers called electron shells.

element: A substance that is made from only one type of atom. Iodine belongs to a group of very reactive elements called the halogens.

equation: an expression using numbers and symbols to explain how a chemical reaction takes place.

ion: A particle of an element similar to an atom but carrying an additional negative or positive electrical charge.

isotopes: Atoms of an element with the same number of protons and electrons but different numbers of neutrons.

laser: A source of light that produces only a single wavelength or color of light.

molecule: A particle that contains atoms held together by chemical bonds.

neutron: A tiny particle with no electrical charge. Neutrons are found in the nucleus of almost every atom.

nucleus: The dense structure at the center of an atom. Protons and neutrons are found inside the nucleus of an atom.

periodic table: A chart containing all the chemical elements laid out in order of their atomic number.

proton: A tiny particle with a positive charge. Protons are found inside the nucleus of an atom.

radioactivity: The release of energy and particles caused by changes in the nucleus of an unstable atom.

reaction: A process in which two or more elements or compounds combine to produce new substances.

saltpeter: Another name for sodium nitrate, a white crystal used in simple explosives.

solute: A substance that dissolves.

solvent: A liquid that can dissolve other substances.

Index